Our Friends Will Pass Among You Silently

DATE DUE

Demco, Inc. 38-293

MAY 1 5 2008

ALSO BY BILL BERKSON

POETRY

Saturday Night: Poems 1960–61
Shining Leaves
Recent Visitors
100 Women
Enigma Variations
Blue Is the Hero
Start Over
Red Devil
Lush Life
A Copy of the Catalogue
Serenade
Fugue State
25 Grand View
Parts of the Body
Same Here

COLLABORATIONS

Two Serious Poems & One Other, with Larry Fagin
Ants, with Greg Irons
Hymns of St. Bridget & Other Writings, with Frank O'Hara
Young Manhattan, with Anne Waldman
What's Your Idea of a Good Time?, with Bernadette Mayer
Gloria, with Alex Katz
Bill, with Colter Jacobson

CRITICISM

The Sweet Singer of Modernism & Other Art Writings 1985 – 2003
Sudden Address: Selected Lectures

EDITOR

Best & Company
Alex Katz, with Irving Sandler
Homage to Frank O'Hara, with Joe LeSueur
What's with Modern Art? by Frank O'Hara

OUR FRIENDS WILL PASS
AMONG YOU SILENTLY

BILL BERKSON

The Owl Press
Woodacre, California 2007

Cover image: Vija Celmins
Night Sky #18, 2000-2001
oil on linen mounted on wood
19 ¾ by 22 ½ inches
Collection the artist.
Courtesy McKee Gallery, New York.
Photo: John Bigelow Taylor.

Design by Margaret Tedesco.

Printed in the United States of America

ISBN 978-0-9669430-8-5

First edition published in 2007 by
The Owl Press
PO Box 126
Woodacre, CA 94973
asisowl@mindspring.com
www.theowlpress.com

The Owl Press is distributed by Small Press Distribution
1341 Seventh Street
Berkeley, California 94710-1403
To order, call 510.524.1668 or toll free 800.869.7553
Fax orders to 510.524.0852
Order via email: orders@spdbooks.org
Order online at www.spdbooks.org

ACKNOWLEDGEMENTS

Versions of some of these poems have appeared in the following publications: *First Intensity, Home, Stolen Island Review, Spectrum, Big Bridge, Home, Floccinancinini-bibipilification, Vanitas, Columbia Review, Joe Brainard, Kaimana, Matrix, Shampoo, Enough, Jacket, Documents Between, Last Night's Dream Corrected, Golden Handcuffs Review, Poieia, Moonlit, San Francisco Art Institute Masters of Fine Arts Exhibition 2005, Fulcrum, Damn the Caesars, Coconut, Chicago Review, Van Gogh's Ear, 88, Sentence, Columbia Review, Yawp, Moonlit, House Organ, Shiny, Mipoesias, Jacket, Whistle, Shuffle Boil, Sal Mimeo, Stolen Island Review, Spectrum*; *Bay Poetics* (Faux Press), *Evidence of the Paranormal* (The Owl Press), and *Fugue State* (Zoland Books, 2001).

The poems in "25 Grand View" appeared variously in *25 Grand View* (San Francisco Center for the Book, 2003) and in *Gloria*, with etchings by Alex Katz (Arion Press, 2005).

Many of the poems in "Same Here" were written for the occasion of a symposium celebrating the exhibition *The Art of Richard Tuttle* at the San Francisco Museum of Modern Art in 2005. Some of those and others appeared as an online chapbook entitled *Same Here* in Big Bridge #11 in January 2006, with illustrations by Nancy Davis.

Liz Rideal originally commissioned "Tango" for her catalogue, *Mandrake Tango* (University Gallery, University of Massachusetts, Amherst).

Auguste Press issued "Gloria" as a broadside in 2001, and a print of "Extreme Patience" was included in the box set *For Tom & Val* (Pressed Wafer, 2004).

"Song for Connie" appeared as a broadside from Narcissus Press, Cambridge, Massachusetts, in April 2006.

An earlier version of "On Certain Pictures by Diane Andrews Hall" appeared in *Diane Andrews Hall* (JG Contemporary/John Berggruen, 2006), and "She Hung Up" in *Carlos Villa: a Retrospective* (Hearst Art Gallery, St. Mary's College, 2007).

Thanks to the editors, publishers and designers of those publications.

Special thanks to Andrew Hoyem, Michael Rothenberg, Mac McGinnes, Greg Sandoval, Duncan McNaughton, Marie Dern, Vija Celmins, David and Renée McKee, Margaret Tedesco, and Albert Flynn DeSilver.

for Connie
and in memory of Michael Stulbarg, M.D.

CONTENTS

25 Grand View

Signature Song

Bunny Berigan first recorded "I Can't Get Started"
with a small group that included Joe Bushkin, Cozy Cole
and Artie Shaw in 1936.
Earlier that same year, the song,
written by Ira Gershwin and Vernon Duke,
and rendered as a duet patter number by Bob Hope and Eve
Arden, made its debut on Broadway in *The Ziegfeld Follies.*
By 1937, when Berigan re-recorded it in a big-band setting,
"I Can't" had become his signature song,
even though, within a few months, Billie Holiday would record
her astonishing version backed
by Lester Young and the rest of the Basie Orchestra.

Lovers for a time, Lee Wiley and Berigan began appearing
together on Wiley's fifteen-minute CBS radio spot,
Saturday Night Swing Club, in 1936.
Berigan died from alcoholism-related causes on June 2, 1942.
Although "I Can't Get Started" is perfectly suited to Wiley's
deep phrasing and succinct vibrato, she recorded the ballad only
once, informally, in 1944, during a Los Angeles club date.
The Spanish Civil War started in 1936 and ended in 1939
with Generalissimo Francisco Franco's forces entering Madrid.
"I've settled revolutions in Spain" goes Gershwin's lyric, just as odd.

Gloria

A large US flag
flaps loudly
outside our dining room,
suspended on a pole
from the topmost balcony
across the way.
                    I keep taking it
for some poor thug
running through the late
September night, sneakers smacking.

Extreme Patience

Of those who, believing the world would end that day, assembled on one member's front porch and sat, waiting in the event that this should occur – it hasn't, and at sunset they get back up and disperse to separate houses until called when next to witness such desirable oblivion.

No Danger of That

Pages from Earth,
glades, furrows, cemetery plots,
a painted band, like a mongoose circling a snake
every half hour

angels of indeterminate
no idea too ingrained
simple glass flash

more violins ahead
far down the enfilade

skyway miracle
issue of durable power
cause for celebration
in time for the next

Cheap Seats

On the telephone answering machine, a sly recorder rendition of "Be it ever so humble there's no place like home."

Similarly, heard at the gym, a country-western singer describing the girl of his dreams as "Picasso-esque."

Once light bounced on the nearby wave. Now it is riddled with troughs. Nope, you are none the wiser, even though the crime is solved, the brat smirks.

Ten Things on the Way to School Today

on assignment for Michael Krouse

The leaves on the tiles inside the front gate. (Windy night.)

An extraordinary, slender, intense woman alighting from her car on Franklin near Oak; when I looked again I saw she had gone to a pay phone on the street.

The pseudo-Gothic church on Franklin and California – it always rings up "beautiful" and "Italy" for me.

Through a window I notice a woman in a black bra working on a computer, her face glowing from the light of the monitor.

The hefty motorcycle cop who sped through the orange roadwork cones at Union Street. What if I had taken the turn around those cones – and the earthmoving machine that blocked my view of him – as quickly as I almost did?

The Chevron station at Union and Van Ness and the two Asian guys who work there goofing in front of the garage lift, and the preponderance of SUVs at the other pumps around me.

A very long white cloud shaped like a hammer.

Signs for "Air Circus" coming up (I forget which day) at Crissy Field.

The confusion of two lanes on the west side of Union at Van Ness, all cars aware that the far side is one lane and that not all cars on the left will signal if turning left.

A woman who looked amazingly like 20-something, blond Riain, but who, when I looked harder, was about 60 years old, waiting for a bus.

Never Happened

Fatal business, near-poems, virtual fatalities
no gloom intended, but see and say
"Morning clouds burning off before noon."

Birds fly in a family of bird life
listed along the chart of the sky.
Where else would sky be

but all around each
peculiar bird, all
optimizing ways of being themselves,

the rest of us inhabiting our typical morass together,
trading sores, consciousnesses, death underwater
(18 men in a Russian tub)

Last Look

Why call it an exit if it spins
Weary of *circa,* plunge I take
Chardin's wife, mortal at her tea

Take, taste, sully your fork

Troublemaker once loved shot his glance,
Rubric on shadow, undifferentiated slices of
The thinner onion

Not What I Thought

The desert, the jungle, the seashore –
Light green meadow ponds release clods glistening runny Vaseline.
Lakeside communities squawk and preen.

Are you hip? Humane?

Minute French birds for dinner, garnish of buckshot bits.
Pork-barrel sour Han emperor outfitted in windowpane burial jade.
That altogether forsaken klepto lady in *Psycho,* Janet Leigh, calling
                                        herself "Marion Crane."

English Suite

"I refuse to take Glenn Gould seriously," she said. But I corrected her: "Not only is Glenn Gould serious, but he is seriously funny." The stony silence that followed saddened me deeply. "I'm sorry it turned out this way," our hostess said, as we went upstairs.

Affair

On the ocean liner deck in *An Affair to Remember,* Deborah Kerr produces the cablegram from her fiancé but the wind grabs it out of her hand. "And *she*, will she be there?" demands Deborah. Cary Grant pats down his tux. No cable, but "Yes," he frowns. Deborah stares into a wave: "We missed our Spring."

Assigned at Will

She said it's like learning to tell time in
a foreign country – you got a
problem with that?

A calcium deposit in deep recesses
puts its chilly finger on the issue.
You neither move nor glow.

She's fumbling with the zipper. No zipper.
The platform proffers a Tuscan sunset
together with petty theft. The time sky does a light feint.

Regency

The Louvre has the best collection.
He died at the Louvre.
Still lifes and genre scenes
In a steamer trunk bound for Boca Raton.

Meanwhile, at the Ecole Pratique des Hautes Etudes
I have to write something understated about how ideas
about art or what life does or won't do clear or not
tend to be lifelike, absurd or preposterous.

Of days among the living these were the most
Teeming with aura of air and purpose.
Between prophecies, we should prefer a glass-bottom boat.

Damages

Number 53, dejected,
mitt in hand
pressed tight against hipbone –

how I gave you away
to those two I no more
care for than

the ball
in zippily fashioned grass
deep right center

Merit

Sorry for the suffering, world,
reaper of sutures, in point of other surface
beneath the silly sheets

What conditions lack is truth
in the absence of conditions
same blank din, soon to be released

Oh boy, oh boy,
the color of your knowing this,
when you do

Tromping through the snow
to see the pictures, cleanly made
by this year's nut

Six Epigrams

"The Anointed Hour"

The Graces came to my door, too –
green bronze next to yellow enamel, mounted
over rows of well-weathered cedar shingles.
I've got to go out for a while, I told them,
make yourselves at home.

Among the Crinolines

A champagne bubble from the 1950s
        in the air still

            What that champagne felt
experienced never forgot deemed
significant   when you cried
            its other bubbles burst

Friends

My friends are ascending,
      inadvertently occupying
positions of importance in the
          contemporary pantheon.
Destiny does things like that.
The rose shimmies with enjoyment over itself.

Plot

There's always a pretty girl in the plot,
but nowadays she calls me "Sir."

A Lady at Her Writing Table

I chose love and friendship over
  work, then
      work and friendship over
    suspended disbelief

            — won't love conquer all?

        I'll never work again.
    Don't call me.

Reimagined Episode

Snack wrappers crinkling down the aisles.
    Cabin pressure dropping
            in the lap of the gods,
                Flushing Meadows.

Bridge

for Willoughby Sharp

William
Holden as
Capt.
Brubaker
USAF, and
his wife
Grace
Kelly saying
(in conjugal
bed, no less)
"Tell me
about the
bridges,
Bru'."
Another era.
Toko-ri.

Heine Song

The rose, the lily, the dove, the sun,
I loved them all in love's mad swoon.
I love them no more, I love only one,
The fine one, lithe one, pure and true;
Selfsame source of all love's flows —
Lily, dove, sun and rose.

Thuringian Equals

Crossed fingers gird the planet, though small optimism obtains.

Will I read *The Serious Doll* in wraps, with its roller slur?

A book where everybody, reader and writer included, dies.

The kind of thing people said in the 1970s: "Hello, I'm back being me again."

My first and last names and the first and last names of both my parents have the same number of letters.

The wasp waist, the tennis dress, the shirtwaist, the dirndl. (Mainbocher)

A distant yet achingly distinct whinny: *et voila!* the walking buckboard.

Dustin Hoffman's bookcase hanging by one hinge in air of Eleventh Street, dawn 1969.

Telephone solicitation for a ballet school in need of "serious floors."

The thought of someone flat on his back on the carpet, tossing and giggling.

If it hurts don't do it. (There are several *unless*es to this caution.)

For the second time in two millennia slept through the meteor shower, results of last night's talk.

After the Medusa

I have to spring lightly to make or thwart a meaning
bare thump at the Safeway's automated door
birds in their vanishing act above or near the U.S. Mint

My mistake, I holler
but poetry comes first
democratizing confluence
despite terror greed

No big deal, larger than life or death
I hear fifes in the outward calm
granite humps and chins
sweet sizeable orpiment
seldom repetitive, un-saying the echo.

Tango

for Liz Rideal

Maybe we need another word for nature
would chaos do
largely friendly lately it has been a confidant
right up there with actuality, another word that insists on being

all leaves and unfigure-out-able turnings
a fork holds up the air sky
its trident mirror image jabs over eons into the
deep dark snuggle

That wanderer's length is a bird-colored
click on deliquescence
shave off the finer hairs
you might find a face

dismissive of skepticism
an opaque residue
where fibers lunch on
circular bugs, or vice versa, affinity, figure and ground

coterminous with
a sapling dressed to the nines to dissemble
launching a lecture or panel discussion
on troubled paradise

lightning strikes but once, as ever from the ground up
I like to sit in its lap
the stellar urgency of this life
actual in less than date and time

Song for Connie

The sun met the moon at the corner
        noon in thin air

Commotion you later
        choose to notice

Love shapes the heart
        that once was pieces

You take in hand
        the heart in mind

Your fate's consistent
        alongside mine

Unless a mess
        your best guess

That is right, thanks, the intimate
        fact that you elect it

At corners, dressed or naked, with lips taste
        full body, time thick or thin, fixated

Love, take heart
        as heart takes shape

And recognition
        ceases to be obscure

One line down the center
        another flying outward enters

Same Here

Tiffany's Song

Once you've been chided often enough
For letting your mind stray far from home,

The sun rises on
Durable moorings.

Squirrel and owl cavort
At the loosened collar of the nasty wood.

The trees grow straight and tall
Around the bend, scribbling rent checks

To absurd obeisance. At the sight of a mouse,
The seasons revert to blended gridlock.

Weird mouse:
Local authorities have found our ship.

Salad Spinner

after Francis Picabia

You must grab time by the hair,
couple subconscious helixes
in the space of a secret.

You must tickle the improbable
and believe in the impossibility
of crossroads.

You must learn to suspend
ten grams of white, five grams of black
in hopes of true scarlet.

You must know how to fall from below
to favor the zenith
of mornings to the manner born.

You must love the four mouths
floating around the silky doubt
of dead assumptions.

For Theremin

Come dusk, the unwary knight steers his swan boat towards a lone spectral damsel despairing grievously on the opposite shore. French horns talk, then cease abruptly. Freeze-dried pathos mounts as evening assumes its calamitous dragon shape. Those scales make explicit an iridescent splurge of spiritual sighting. Slender willows exchange *pensées,* arriving apace at the shared understanding that self-help is as useless and impenetrable as the blanket arbitrariness of class determinations.

"I thought they were beautiful but they're really glamorous."

(Bruce Conner on Nathaniel Dorsky's films)

Philip Whalen directs failed eyes toward the whirring Bolex.
Between thumb and forefinger the perceptual moment clicks:
"The camera is the world. I love the world."

Bright Soul

How about a can of Coke?
Yes and no.
Kenneth Koch.

Glass Hoist

The dictates of history are not of this world.
Plentitude and transcendent artifice
Unhinge the gates.

Overlooked commonalities remain negotiable
Upheld by those whose sense of touch
Runs counter to the claim of vision altogether.

But Then

Nobody knows
the trouble – the wasted
whistles, catcalls, oceanic blitz,

       diehard
     push-button
   fashion-conscious
     expressivity.

Our Friends Will Pass Among You Silently

You hope the Earth is equitable,
Because why else are you here,
Fraught with the extra time
And surefire energy, clear
And in the same breath, not.

Garbage, detritus, commandeers
Much of each day,
But materiality doesn't look that way to a peanut
Nor yet at us, prey as we seem to be
To the intimate void granted to assuage the even bigger abyss without.

Beams keep solvent if unpolished in
Amassed yearly vaultings.
Crumbs and contouring in an antique frame
Compound the sands they shift and bear the foot
Traffic along its jagged route.

Old Walkway, you who are traditionally mistaken about
Your portion of this well-whittled master plan,
How phenomena lodge
In every filter and grander
Conceptions dance the Life-form Jack.

Sorry about what passes as fact
In emboldened dot patterns, extended fingerings
Like Norway's prettiest tree
Against clouds' residual entertainment brought home
To meet our obligations as pockets fail.

For Per Henrik Wallin

Intentionality, can't hear you for the din

    no sound in sight, inheritance

        if listening is endearment, but impervious

           a liberty positioned tight

    in the still of the night

a handful of stars

Art Diary

for David Meltzer

Estes looks good here
Celmins exquisite,
and everything about that Brillo Box
achieves its lucent quiddity in time.

A New-Age showboat
of vinyl and kapok,
lithe bodies and retroactive fruit
film a sense of being at the event.

All are "expressions," each a ritual trick
with multiple crotch marks, lineaments,
cultural signage like metaphoric cleft chins
and precepts beyond

their facial contours. In a dark map,
Government Dog bites Everyman's butt,
and the worry lines on Mother's
brow deepen.

Remember when cognition could walk and talk
and copyright desire?
True, art today won't work like that —
funny-peculiar, not ha-ha.

A.K.A. The Pantheon is Flooded

If only you had had the pep,
History would have been altered by your step.

Puttering in the poetry patch,
Inspirational, but here's the catch:

The copy editor hasn't called,
My pet worry's fraught with holes.

Plotting, patterning, preface confused –
The milk seemed all right but then curdled at

The boiling point, a Vermeer sort of melt,
Viscous velocity of borderline. All

These books that poets fill while I
Trepass as a pigeon might,

Banana in exhaust pipe, light brown on top,
White below.

Bearing honeycomb externals.
We had just pulled up at the curb when

Inspired, I threw down the book, turgid trash heap,
Fount of useless information, sexually explicit

But nevertheless alone.

Compass Points

All over herself
Thing said to my face
Blank of luster
To which ledges speak

Thing said
Correct objective
With slight bias
You or your dog

Oh disturb
The kettle to Edvard Munch
Assembly of ditches
Horizon asserts

You or the dog year
Dumped by the seaside
Pudding the sun never soaks
Beggars events

How quickly absorb, spoken cabal
Over moist mist recital
Slips ultimately left vertical of her being
Blistering, sea starts, brought, you tease

Cuban Fives

for Kit Robinson

Time the sound of what is more
Look sharp allow this clunk
Heady malice
Odd items situational is affect, loan
Just as "lusts" make clear mimetic physics

One question is traditional
What did the lady forget? or did you leave behind?
If anything, mature clowns stare
Create for press shots
Tidy inertia astounding remains he builds

Please acknowledge
There is music there too
Especially in some of Mahler's 7th
The viewer's headgear and little teeth
Rolling down on Salsa Sue

Wait for nature's tsk
Take the bait for lunar task
Last flowers doom nowadays arctic mull
Kiss-off kiss closet language leagues
And the horrid roll remains

States listings classes principles codes
Lumbar classics of a blue tin enameled bucket lakeside
But at maneuvers you stayed
Soft under the pout fumes
Events outer to mind beckoned

Militant male member
Pound of the ocean kit
I tell my friends
That's the end
Gifted female elements knocking

Just a phase at midday
Like money in the bank
Enormous portion ruined
Thirty seconds in love
Carved in animal court

And attendant crypts
An Alp's reunion here, but there
Rides negative ecstasy
User perfect,
Creep

A clitoris stuck to the tongue
Expenditure's private
Smatter of taste
For beans and sub clauses
Accommodating the spectral nozzle

Spelling integral pecks on the cheek
A straw person I once had
Occasion to observe
All-out attack on a one-of-a-kind
One of those on a heave

Tuna shoes
Suction the nonce
Everything on a windy day
Hooting through the brush
It is spring in the desert

As married people do
With mangled saints
Call of white heart
Loss
Once the remedial shelf

It is Easter in the phenomena
Each wandering soul
Open to suggestion
And the night sky less confounded afterwards
New grass with old

Which is why a soul kiss
Beetle Bailey pounds the mess hall counter
With Sarge's head
Insubordination
Azalea, either way a time-worn mesh

Phosphanes dabble in a field guide
For dead elephants
Tangents pour afoot
With hemoglobin on the way
Engender feats of caution

How operative
A doorstep on a star
High-definition clouds
One lung two tongue
Each thread a cluster into package slant

Without Penalty

As Traffic School becomes the ruling
Paradigm of higher learning

And the citizenry pays dearly
For the right to witness ex-CHP officers engaged

In fitfully polishing
Their monologues, hopeful, at best,

Of high-end careers
On late-night Cable,

It's not so much the shame inflicted
As the concomitant displays

Of the eternal drunken car chase divided
By Infinity's irradiated speed bumps,

Careening en route
To regime change, permanent and without end.

Goods and Services

Are you a 15th-century Italian monk of present-day ill repute?
No, I am not Savonarola.

Whenever anyone steals something it is Prometheus
But theft is ascribed to Hermes.

Word went out that the missing husband had been found
Behind his house, washing his pants.

My class notes are illegible.
Code name: "Clemency."

In Costume

The endangered energy guys are coming on a Monday
And the steamed-up picture window (time being what it is, its prolonged
Disconnect elaborately personified) wavers blue-ishly spotlit,
Affecting a slight concussion to face the styptic deer.

In the parlance of permanence many bulbs need replacing.
I heard the woods speaking but they went about it the wrong way around,
Panting like mutts in the leafy strata.
Unlikely lunch: Dark toast soaked in soup du jour.

Agnes Morehead, Goddess of Nimbly Erected Spite, tell us,
What is it that will make life palatable when so it is?
And lunch absorbs from light executive privilege
At the high end of the cerebral cortex afloat on my fiery palatial plank.

She flies! The saucer can't *not* act.
The clock is whole, its animations invariably tingling,
Recruited to receive pronouncement of the final
Anagram hastily received dark nights long before graduation.

A Recording Device

Well, back to my ablutions then.
You never walk in the same movie
twice or feel the traction between
experience's proprietary sleepless
light pervading the girder's
                         unclouded eye.

You will want to lap the sheen off anyone's personal orifice
to imagine vapors crossing the grid's white string
                  wrapped
around a rusty nail, sweet denim moon swallowed up,
              coercing landscape lovers
                    articulated.
          Between action-packed earth
              and acquisitive skies
                    there's a job to be done:
              spatial distances
          simply minding parked cars
       in suspicious places – the shrine of matter, perhaps
              ephemeral yet.

On Certain Pictures by Diane Andrews Hall

The cumulus swells, depending,
Aged or ageless, and one thin pink tousle
Crosses its dark denser other, seeking

To learn of the ample ones
Allow for two, permit descriptive –
Then square the merger by combing a detail.

Smitten like sea strata, the view
Of "breakers" feeds the rise, the steep lilt to join,
Glory wash abut to top-right billow-and-fluff brigades.

You find clinchers deep in white noise,
A reef of focus sustaining
Ocean's overbite.

Perceived against the eerily orange
Neon zinnia, the exquisite goldfinch
Takes naked nerve.

The surround – Sensibility, you can smell it in a flash!
Synaptic hole punch, dire pinch of the Greater Photon:
My mind has a flash wound.

The flowery instant flits,
Gone chuckling, rinsed
Down the fabled lane.

Daylight on a wall inspected
Enlarges to plank-like angles –
You go there, mentally, refracted.

Light shows the way the day goes,
And if distinction follows the sense of it
Can be only gratitudinous.

A child of this shimmer,
Swimming as fast as I can,
Paddling that summer, I fell down.

A painting's squared-off bloom of surface apprehending,
Ordinary, caught, aligned, benign,
Neither literal nor not, and not a mirror, after all.

She Hung Up

for Carlos Villa

Shadows fall from bricks
In the line of fire without a song
You do the math
People talk and carry on

In the line of fire without a song
An escalator cannot divide
People talk and carry on
Esperanto etudes at Weather Wall

An escalator cannot divide
Many pink petals in a vortex of Oreos
Esperanto etudes at Weather Wall
What gravity is, knowing how the light

Many pink petals in a vortex of Oreos
Earth tones escape the citrus ouch
What gravity is, knowing how the light
Like Russian theft comes minimal, minimized

Earth tones escape the citrus. "Ouch,
Love is a loading dock
Like Russian theft" comes minimal, minimized
In/ out, in/ out, in/ out – but only somewhat slightly

Love is a loading dock
She hung up
In/ out, in/ out, in/ out – but only somewhat slightly
A bouquet of crates

She hung up
They were flint chippers in high school
A bouquet of crates
Quel drôle de vie of Green Card agapanthus

They were flint chippers in high school
Your tentative liabilities awesome as a news hour
Quel drôle de vie of Green Card agapanthus
Let the sunniness of Classicism shine

Your tentative liabilities awesome as a news hour
Shadows fall from bricks
Let the sunniness of Classicism shine
You do the math

Poem Beginning with a Remark by Richard Tuttle

One remarkable phenomenon of my work is its love for being hung at a height of fifty-four inches from the floor . . . This height brings me in contact with anything that's ever existed in human life.

— R.T. 2001/2004

Sudden outbursts may be key
So Fred Rain quipped to Henry Rust
As the diamantes fell from her veil
In Part Two of *Les Enfants du Paradis:*
Dear Waste for Good,
As far as time and tide may go
This far have I admired
The penis-fashioned clouds
Pressing on her jugular
Schlepp the multiple joule sessions of
In ripened snow
Drip nymph case spun
Such is life's felicity
Within foulard accompaniments
Superhuman venues (e.g., "sites")
Things will keep, keep them
At rest, environmentally
Speaking of catwalks
Suspension of plumb line
Compatible pocket auras
Stacked exegesis
Something an anemone can relate
The wanderer in you
Little Lulu
Eye fool
Hath remained intact
Among dried-out figs
The miniature minister is reproved
In the funnel, funnily enough, you fuck

In sneer quotes
For what is never to be clear in any case
Sexuality gorgeous to a fault
Wiping up
Because just stepping out into sunlight
October, first of several arbitrary dates
The tiger in its nimble meekness is no less light than I
I'm . . .
Sanity's surface work
Live column of water
And everything in it alive, as well
But beware, stumped starling, khaki saint
Or get you darkening beyond your ken
"Ziggernaut" orbiting *Sartor Resartus*
Aestheticism detachment parallel to shock
Stepping water
That softens the heart
You could photograph something, anything, instead
You could be empty or dead
And get away or by – a by-product of light
And mud
Don't forget to alternate
Besides, how have we done this?
Hand by foot
A miracle
Not to mention air
A crush went forth
Sounds furthered the thought
What it might stay for
Because to work is surface
Things will be here, then back
With luminosity appended
The rest is ditto
Sight unseen, admit it

The Way We Live Now

*I had a meeting with a senior advisor
to Bush. He expressed the White
House's displeasure, and then he told me
something that at the time I
didn't fully comprehend
but which I now believe gets to
the very heart of
the Bush presidency.
The aide said that guys like me
were "in what we call
the reality-based community,"
which he defined as
people who "believe that
solutions emerge from
your judicious study of
discernible reality."
I nodded and murmured something about
enlightenment principles and empiricism.
He cut me off.
"That's not the way the world
really works anymore,"
he continued. "We're an empire now,
and when we act, we create
our own reality.
And while you're studying
that reality — judiciously, as you will —
we'll act again, creating
other new realities,
which you can study too, and that's
how things will sort out.
We're history's actors ...
and you, all of you, will be left
to just study
what we do."*